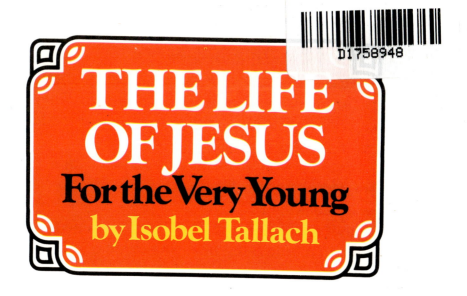

THE LIFE OF JESUS
For the Very Young
by Isobel Tallach

Illustrated by
Lawrence Littleton Evans

THE BANNER OF TRUTH TRUST

Mary and Joseph had travelled a long way. They were glad to reach Bethlehem.

They went to the inn at Bethlehem. But the inn was full; there was no room left for them. They had to go to a stable, where animals stay, to find a place to sleep.

The stable was for cows and donkeys. In it there was a manger filled with straw for the animals to eat.

In that stable a wonderful thing happened. Mary had a little baby boy. She made a bed for him in the manger and she called him Jesus.

Jesus was different from any other baby that there ever was. His mother was Mary, but his father was not Joseph. His father was God.

It was dark all over Bethlehem. In the stable Mary and Joseph watched over the new baby.

That same night, in a field near Bethlehem, some shepherds were looking after their sheep. Suddenly, out of the darkness, a light shone all around them. It was an angel, and the light around him was beautiful and so bright that the shepherds were afraid.

But the angel said to them, 'Do not be afraid, because I am bringing you good news. Jesus is born in Bethlehem.'

All at once the shepherds saw many more angels. They were all full of joy because Jesus was born ; they were all singing together.

As soon as the angels had gone the shepherds said to one another, 'Let us go into Bethlehem to see him for ourselves.'

They left their sheep and hurried off to Bethlehem to find the baby.

They were glad to see him. They were glad that he was called Jesus because Jesus means *someone who saves.*

Joseph made a home for Mary and Jesus in the little town of Nazareth and they all lived there together.

Quite a long way from Jesus' home was a city called Jerusalem. Every year there were special services in Jerusalem, and many people went there to go to church. Only, they called their church the Temple.

When Jesus was twelve he went there too, with Mary and Joseph, and they stayed in Jerusalem for a few days.

At last Joseph and Mary set off for home. Many people walked along the road with them. They thought Jesus was there too. Then night time came. Time to stop and get ready to sleep. But Joseph and Mary could not find Jesus anywhere. They had to go all the way back to Jerusalem to look for him. There they searched and searched until at last they found him in the temple. Jesus loved the temple because it was God's house and God was his Father.

Jesus was a man now. He left his home in Nazareth and went from place to place, preaching and helping people.

One day a nobleman came to Jesus for help. He was rich and he had a lovely home, but he was sad. His little boy was sick, so sick that he was going to die.

The nobleman said to Jesus, 'Please come home with me and heal my little boy.'

But Jesus did not need to go home with him. He could heal the little boy, even though he was not standing beside his bed or touching him. And he did heal him right then, from where he was, a long way from the sick boy's home.

Then Jesus said to the nobleman, 'Just go home now. Your little boy is all right.' The nobleman believed Jesus and went home. He found his little boy strong and well again.

Jesus said:

Anyone who listens to me and does what I say is like a wise man who built his house on a rock.

First, he dug down into the earth. He dug until he reached the rock. Then he began to build. He built up his house on the rock.

When it was finished, a storm came. The wind blew hard and the rain poured down. It poured down until the water ran in streams along the ground and beat against the house.

But the house stood firm and safe because it was built on the rock.

Then Jesus said:

Anyone who listens to me but does not do what I say is like a foolish man who built his house on the sand.

He built his house quickly and easily. He did not dig down to the rock. But the storm came against his house too. The rain got heavier and heavier. The wind blew louder and louder. Rushing streams of water beat and beat and beat against the house. The walls began to crack, then they began to lean over. At last the house fell flat to the ground with a terrible crash. It fell because it was only built on sand.

On the Sabbath days Jesus went to the synagogue. The synagogue was a kind of church.

One day he saw a man there with a withered hand. The hand was quite useless. The man couldn't stretch it out, or eat with it, or do anything with it.

Jesus felt sorry for him. He knew he could heal that man. Jesus said to him, 'Stand up'. And the man stood up.

Everyone was watching him and everyone was waiting to see what Jesus would do.

Then Jesus said, 'Stretch out your hand'. This was the very thing the poor man could not do. But Jesus healed him so that he could stretch it out. And his hand was perfectly healed. It was as good and strong as his other hand.

Jesus chose some special friends to go with him as he went from place to place. They were called disciples.

One day Jesus and his disciples started crossing the Sea of Galilee in a boat. Jesus was very tired. He lay down in the boat with his head on a pillow and fell asleep.

Then suddenly a storm blew up over the sea. The sky grew dark and the wind blew harder and harder. Huge waves tossed around the boat. And then the wind blew the waves so hard that they came splashing right into the boat.

The disciples were very scared. They felt sure the boat would sink. They went to Jesus and woke him up.

Jesus stood up in the boat and spoke to the wind and the waves. He said, 'Peace, be still'. And the wind stopped howling and the waves stopped tossing and everything was very still.

The disciples were amazed. They said to one another, 'What kind of man is this, that even the wind and the sea obey him?'

In the land where Jesus was, a little girl and her mother and father lived happily together. But one day sadness came to their home. The little girl became sick. As time passed, she got worse and worse.

Her father, whose name was Jairus, was so worried about her that he hurried off to find Jesus. He asked Jesus to come and heal his little girl, so Jesus started walking with him back along the road to Jairus' home.

As they walked along the road someone came from Jairus' home to meet them. He brought sad news. The little girl had died.

But Jesus did not turn back. He and Jairus walked on to the house, and went into the room where the little girl was lying.

Jesus took her hand in his and said, 'Little girl, get up.' And she got up and walked.

How very surprised her mother and father were, but how very, very happy!

One day Jesus and his disciples went to a quiet place where nobody lived. A big crowd of people followed him there. All day long Jesus preached to them and healed the ones who were sick.

Towards the end of the day everyone began to feel hungry. They wanted something to eat, but they had no food with them.

Then someone found a boy in the crowd who had brought some food. He had five little loaves of bread and two small fishes. That was just enough food for himself, though. It wasn't nearly enough to feed all those men and women and children.

But Jesus could make it enough to feed them. He told the disciples to make the people sit down on the grass. Then he took the little boy's loaves and fishes in his hands. He looked up to heaven and thanked God for them. Then he gave them to his disciples, and they went among the people, handing them out.

There was enough for everyone. There was so much food that there was even some left over.

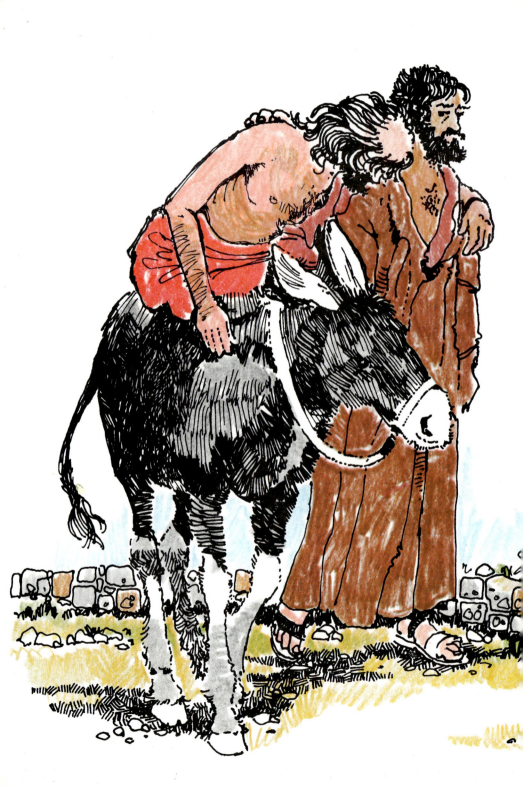

Jesus told this story:

A man once walked on his own along a lonely rocky road. Suddenly thieves jumped out on him. They hit him; then they took away all he had, even his clothes. After that, they just left him where he was, lying hurt at the side of the road. He was bleeding, and he badly needed help.

Someone came. But he didn't help. He passed by on the other side of the road.

Then another man came along. He crossed the road to look at the poor hurt man, but he didn't help either. He just went on down the road.

At last someone else came, a Samaritan with a donkey. He felt sorry for the wounded man. He poured oil and wine into his wounds and bandaged them up gently. Then he lifted him up and put him on his own donkey. He took him to an inn and took care of him there.

The next day the Samaritan had to go away, but he took out some money and gave it to the innkeeper. He asked the innkeeper to go on looking after the sick man until he was better.

Jesus said that we should be kind to others, as the Samaritan was.

This is another story Jesus told:

There was once a boy who was very selfish. One day he said to his father, 'Father, give me some money.' His father gave him the money. The boy then packed up all his things, took his money, and went off to a country far away.

In that country he bought everything he wanted until he had no money left. No money for clothes, no money even for food. Soon he had only ragged clothes to wear, and he was very hungry.

He got work to do, feeding pigs. But he was still so hungry he even wanted to eat the food he was giving to the pigs.

He was miserable. He knew he had done wrong. He knew his father might be very angry with him. But the only thing he could think of doing was going home and saying how sorry he was.

Slowly and sadly he started trudging home.

He was still a long way from home when his father saw him coming. Instead of being angry, his father ran to meet him and put his arms round him and kissed him. He got him the best clothes and the best food, and took his boy into his own home again.

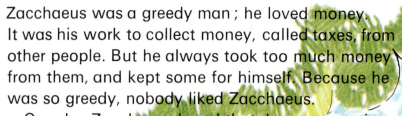

Zacchaeus was a greedy man; he loved money.
It was his work to collect money, called taxes, from
other people. But he always took too much money
from them, and kept some for himself. Because he
was so greedy, nobody liked Zacchaeus.

One day Zacchaeus heard that Jesus was going
to pass through his town. Many people in the
town went out into the streets to see Jesus.

Zacchaeus went too. But Zacchaeus was a small man, and he could not see over the people who stood in front of him.

Then Zacchaeus had an idea. He ran and climbed up a tree by the side of the road. Now he was higher than anybody else; now he could see Jesus very well.

He watched Jesus walking along the road. Then Zacchaeus got a big surprise. Jesus stopped under the tree and looked up at him. And Jesus spoke to him; Jesus spoke to the greedy little man whom nobody liked.

'Come down!' Jesus said to him. 'Today I am going to visit your house.'

Zacchaeus climbed quickly down the tree and took Jesus to his house. He was very happy that Jesus would come to his home.

After Jesus' visit Zacchaeus was quite different. He wasn't greedy any more. He gave back money he shouldn't have taken from people, and he gave away his own money to poor people. He didn't love money any more. Now he loved Jesus instead.

One evening, just as it was getting dark, Jesus and his disciples met in an upstairs room in Jerusalem.

Gently Jesus began to tell his disciples something that made them very sad. He told them the time had come for him to leave them. He was going to die. It was not that he was going to become sick, and die in that way. But wicked men would come and take him away to kill him. Jesus was going to let those men kill him for a very special reason.

In that upstairs room they were all sitting around a table. On the table there was bread and wine. Jesus took the bread. He thanked God for it, then he broke it into pieces and gave the pieces to his disciples to eat. He told them that, just as the bread had been broken, so his body was going to be broken too.

Then he took the cup of wine and gave it to the disciples to drink. He said that, just as the wine had been poured out, so his blood was going to be poured out too.

Jesus left that upstairs room and went down to a garden. There the wicked men came and found him. They tied his hands and took him away.

The men took Jesus to a place called Calvary. They had with them a big wooden cross. They nailed Jesus to the cross. They put nails in his hands and feet, and set the cross up in the ground. His blood poured down. He hung there for a time and then he died.

Now here is the special reason why Jesus died in that way. Everyone in the world has done wrong, and no-one is good enough to live with God in Heaven. Jesus came into the world to die, not for himself, but for those who had done wrong. Now each one who loves Jesus can go to be with God in Heaven.

After Jesus died, all his friends were very sad. Two of them took down his body from the cross. They carried it to a garden where there was a cave. They laid Jesus' body there and rolled a big stone up to the front of the cave to close it. After that they went home, sadder than they had ever been in their lives before.

Then, early one morning, one of Jesus' friends came to that cave where his body lay. Her name was Mary Magdalene. She was surprised to find that the big stone had been rolled away from the front of the cave. And the cave was empty ; Jesus' body was not there any more.

Mary did not know that Jesus was alive again. She thought that someone had taken his body away, and she stood outside the cave and cried.

Then she saw someone standing near her. He spoke to her, but she did not know who he was. He said to her, 'Mary'. When she heard him say her name, then she knew who he was. It was Jesus.

How happy she was to see Jesus, and to hear him speak to her again ! And how gladly she ran to find the sad disciples. She had such wonderful news to tell them—Jesus was alive again !

Later that day, the disciples were together in a room in Jerusalem. Mary had told them that Jesus was alive again, but they thought it could not be true. They were still sad.

The doors of their room were shut. But all of a sudden they saw Jesus himself standing in the room beside them. They could hardly believe that it was Jesus. He spoke to them, and showed them the marks of the nails in his hands and feet. Then they knew that it really was Jesus, and they were very glad.

That day, and in the days afterwards, Jesus often talked to the disciples. He told them that very soon he would be going back to his Father in Heaven. But he told them that he would still be near them too.

Then, one day, Jesus took his disciples out of the city of Jerusalem to a quiet place. He lifted up his hands and blessed them. And while he was blessing them he was carried up into Heaven.

They watched him until they could see him no longer. But they were not sad. They knew that he was near them still, although they could not see him.

They walked back to Jerusalem as happy as could be.